Moss Ball
Bonsai

100 Beautiful Kokedama
That are Fun to Create

Satoshi Sunamori

TUTTLE Publishing

Tokyo | Rutland, Vermont | Singapore

Table of Contents

PART
1

Having Fun with Moss Balls

Plants have the power to subtly ease our anxieties, and growing plants brings us closer to nature. In this book we'll introduce you to the joy of bringing plants together with moss to make unique moss ball gardens.

The Power of Moss

1

Making and Sustaining the Forest

Moss is known to be one of the earliest life forms on the planet. Unlike other plants, moss doesn't use vascular tissues to transport water and nutrients, but instead absorbs everything directly through the leaves and stems. With this special ability, moss can live as long as it has light and moisture.

There are thousands of different types of moss on the planet. Moss has many purposes in the ecosystem and it's very resilient. For example, when there's a wildfire, the first thing to grow back is moss. The spore is easily carried to different places, allowing moss to migrate great distances. Even without dirt, moss is able to grow. Eventually, wherever moss grows, a forest follows.

1. Polytrichum growing thickly on a dead tree trunk. 2. Cedar sprouting out of a moss-covered trunk. 3. A tree that sprouted from a moss-covered stone. The moss on the stone can be seen as a nurturer of new life.

Moss also maintains the forest's humidity by collecting rainwater, thereby keeping nutrients and dirt from ebbing away. In addition, reproduction of other life forms such as insects depends on moss. These are just some of the ways our ecosystem relies on moss.

The layer of moss nourishes new sprouting trees and also protects it from fungi invasion. Unlike soil, it houses no grass to prevent light from reaching the sprout. This is an ideal set up to raise a seed to the first sprout.

For sure, the forest can't exist without moss.

It's symbiosis!

Heart-shaped leaves make it extra lovely. Katsura moss ball (p. 78).

Add a Bit of Nature to Your Home

Kokedama (*koke-*=moss; *dama*=ball) is a work of bonsai art. Moss found its way into the making of bonsai long ago, and it's no wonder. The level of precipitation in Japan is higher than average in comparison to other countries, making the climate very suitable for moss—Japan grows about 1800 different types!

Moss is used in bonsai in various ways. A moss ball is a carefree, light-hearted kind of gardening, and making moss balls is something that anyone can enjoy doing.

Put simply, with kokedama, moss takes the place of a pot. You can enjoy a different sort of aesthetic with this style of planting. Your plants are displayed as they would appear straight from the forest or garden—simple and completely natural.

Mountain Hydrangea moss ball (p. 69).
A combination with Spike moss.

Getting Started

It is easy to create a moss ball if you have all the right tools and ingredients. At garden shops you'll find a huge variety of plants in progress. Just choose the one you'd like to grow inside a moss ball—and there's no need to stop at just one.

For starters, you should choose a plant that's easy to grow and care for, either from a garden shop or from your own yard (see How to Make Moss Balls starting on p. 16).

3

1

Some examples for starters:
1. Hinoki moss ball (p. 80).
2. Paper Cascade moss ball (p. 63).
3. Fern moss ball.
4. Solomon's Seal moss ball (p. 85).

4

2

1. Columbine moss ball with driftwood (p. 62). 2. Hanging vines of Morning Glory moss ball (p. 72). 3. Moss on moss ball. Japanese Climacium moss ball (p. 94).

Creative Ways to Display

Having a moss ball in your home adds a little character to your living space. When you become more skillful at creating moss balls you can do many things to jazz them up. You can try hanging them or tweak the shapes a little (p. 31). You can even try several different plants together.

Growing Just Moss

Another way to have fun with mosses is to simply grow them in glass containers (p. 43). If there's a lid to your container, you can easily grow it in your room. Moss also makes a fun and unusual gift.

1. Multiple mosses started from Japanese dried moss, planted in a glass container. 2. Japanese Climacium moss in a medicine jar. 3. Hinoki moss growing in a jar. 4. Juniper haircap in a jar, seen from above.

Part 1
Having Fun with Moss Balls

How to Make Moss Balls

Haigoke moss ball

Yamagoke moss ball

Haigoke

Yamagoke

Brachythecium Moss moss ball

Shinobu Goke moss ball

What Kinds of Moss are Suitable for Making Moss Balls?

Sphagnum works well for most kinds of moss balls. For a more authentic bonsai/Japanese moss garden feel, specialty mosses that grow in different parts of Japan are available in bonsai shops and online.

① Haigoke is probably the most popular option. Because of its matte texture it is easy to form a ball and is relatively resistant to dryness. ② Yamagoke moss (Japanese mountain moss) is a bonsai favorite, used as topdressing for plants that like a bit of acidic soil (like azaleas). Like Haigoke, it is also resistant to dryness. ③ Others… Thuidium faces the shade, and requires humidity, but the moss holds together well so it's easy to form a ball. Brachythecium is a moss that grows on soil, rock and bark. The matte texture makes it easy to work with.

Where to Get Mosses for Kokedama?

Haigoke and Yamagoke moss can sometimes be found at bonsai specialty stores or from online retailers. Online vendors that specialize in moss are a good source.

Moss can be purchased in various forms, from kits that will provide enough moss for a couple of kokedama, to moss plant starters, to sheets of 5 pounds (2.5 k) or more.

Pack size of Haigoke (above) and yamagoke (bottom).

Fuji Sand
1

Keto Soil
1

Akadama Soil
1

Property of Soil	When using "Musou"	Without "Musou"
Soil with good drainage and proper humidity	Just Musou	Keto Soil 1: Fuji Sand 1
Soil with good drainage	Musou 1: Fuji Sand 1 (or pebbles)	Akadama soil 1: Fuji Sand 1

What Kinds of Soil Should be Used for Moss Balls?

In general, keto soil is good for moss balls because its clay-like properties allow the soil to hold together. On the other hand, keto soil tends to dry up quickly and doesn't absorb moisture as well, so it usually doesn't perform well on its own.

In this book, we will mostly recommend using a combination of pebbles and soil. For some bonsai we have used a soil called Musou, a Japanese product formulated specifically for moss ball gardening. Musou has the ability to conserve moisture while providing good drainage, and so can be used on is own. If you cannot yet find Musou in your region or online, you can combine keto soil as a connecting base with akadama soil and Fuji sand.

Musou soil designed for moss ball gardening.

Basic Forms

Here we will use Haigoke moss to form a moss ball. Once you learn the basics, you should be able to get creative with other projects.

--- WHAT TO PREPARE ---

Plant (here we are using Hatsuyukikazura), Haigoke, soil (here we are using Musou), a roll of string, tweezers.

Preparation

1 Moisten the moss. To help ensure it holds together later on, make a cut into the center.

2 Cut off any dried up bits from the moss.

3 Wet the soil you've prepared and knead the soil well.

Start

1. Take the plant out of the pot, and massage the root ball to remove excess soil and free up the root.

2. With the wet soil you've prepared, evenly form a layer of soil around the roots. While kneading out the air pockets, use both hands to squeeze the soil to form a tight ball.

3. Without burying the stem, shape the soil into a nice round shape. Make sure the ball can be set to stand up straight. Shape the base accordingly.

4. Cover the soil ball with the moss sheet you've prepared. If possible, arrange the moss so that ends don't overlap. If they do overlap, cut off the excess portion.

5. Shape the ball with both hands.

6. Use the string to reinforce the ball from different angles.

\ And it's done! /

7. After wrapping the string around about 10 times, leave 4" (10 cm) of string, and cut. You can use the pliers to pin the string to the bottom of the ball with a U-shape wire.

8. Once you're done securing the ball, water it! In addition to providing needed moisture, watering clears away unwanted debris. You can also soak the ball in water.

When the Plant Requires Good Drainage

Plants such as succulents require soil with good drainage. It is difficult to form a ball if the soil contains just Fuji sand and light pebbles. You can mix in some Musou to help with cohesion. If you don't have Musou, you can form a ball with gauze and tie it with string. Then cover the gauze-formed ball with moss (refer to images 1–4).

★ When making a succulent moss ball, it's fine to use just small pebbles in your gauze wrap.

Making a Moss Ball with Yamagoke Moss

Using Yamagoke moss requires a bit of know-how. First of all, you must wet the moss with plenty of water, otherwise the moss will immediately peel off. The moisture also allows the string to wrap around much easier, keeping it all together. Keeping this in mind will help prevent failed attempts.

 Start

1 Wrap soil around the roots of the plant, and shape it into a ball (as shown in the steps on p. 18). This plant is Chinese Virginia Creeper.

2 Wet the moss and start laying it on the soil.

3 Add moss to all parts but the bottom. Press on firmly, so there are no gaps, and until the ball is firm.

4 Wrap some string around 2–3 times until the moss is fastened to the ball of soil.

5 Add moss to the bottom of the ball.

6 Fasten the added moss with some string. Then continue from step 7 shown on p. 19.

\ And it's done! /

Combining Several Plants

You can enjoy a more complex and colorful moss ball by adding flowering and non-flowering plants together. Before making your first one, read through the following steps to see how easy it is to do.

Start ▷

1 This example combines Chinese Tallow and Asamarindou. Moss and soil preparation is on p. 16.

2 Take both the plants out of the original pot, and gently remove soil off the roots.

3 Decide how you would like to arrange the plants. The recommended rule is to have the shorter plant in front of the taller one.

4 Start pressing the two plants together.

5 Then start adding soil around the roots to create a ball.

\ And it's done! /

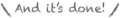

6 Press the soil into a tight ball.

7 Make sure the bottom of the ball is flat enough so the ball can be set upright. Then continue from step 4 shown on p. 19.

Having Fun with Moss Balls

Enjoying Growth

When the moss ball is newly formed, the string is quite visible. Over time, the string becomes less and less visible as new moss grows over it. You'll also notice that whereas the dried moss you started out with would have been somewhat brownish, your moss ball becomes beautifully green when the new moss grows in.

Newly made moss ball: the wrapping string is visible.

1 month later

One month later: the wrapping string is no longer visible, as beautiful new greenery grows over it.

Enjoy Transformation After Bloom

For moss balls with flowers as a center, once the flower wilts, the joy shouldn't just stop there. The flower once in bloom will transition into its next form. It is as the moss ball has transformed. You can also try striking (cloning) the plant (p. 34), or combine with other plants.

Once the Jeffersonia Dubia flower is has withered, you can still enjoy the green that follows.

Once the Red Spider Lily has bloomed, the stem wilts, and the leaves sprout.

Enjoying the Weeds

As you grow your moss ball, weeds will sprout here and there. Seeds of weeds could have snuck into your moss or your plant from the beginning. If your plant came from out of doors, the inclusion of weeds would be natural and normal. You can let weeds serve as a feature in your moss ball. If you don't care for weeds, you can always trim them off.

Water Willow sprouted, adding little flowers to the moss ball.

Creeping Woodsorrow sprouting from the side, adding some accent.

The Mushrooms on Your Moss Ball

During the more humid seasons, mushrooms tend to appear. It would be nice if these were something like Shiitakes, but the mushrooms growing from moss balls are usually tiny ones. After just a few days, the mushrooms will disappear, so keep an eye out.

A colony of orange mushrooms sprouting from a moss ball.

White mushroom sprouting from a moss ball.

Go by the Seasons

Depending on the plants you grow, your collection, or even just one moss ball, can give you something to enjoy year round. Flowers in spring, fresh green leaves in summer, red leaves in the fall, and so on.

Cherry Blossom moss ball in April, and then fresh new leaves two months later.

Hazelnut in August, then in late fall.

Kuranperi- and Giboushi combo moss ball in later June. Then in early November it sports a fruity red color.

How to Care for Moss Balls

I need TLC

Placement and Lighting

The best place to keep your moss ball is outdoors on a porch or in a garden. Make sure to not place it near any sort of exhaust fan, such as an air conditioning window unit, since the wind from the fan will weaken the moss. In fact, avoid strong wind altogether. Don't place the moss directly on concrete and so on. These substances absorb summer heat that could kill the moss. Moss is happy with about half a day's worth of sunlight, and plenty of time in the shade as well.

That said, you must also consider the needs of the plants contained in the moss ball. Plants that require a lot of light can be placed out in the light for most of the day. In spring and fall when the moss is at its optimal growth, plants that prefer less light can take indirect sunlight. Summer is when moss balls endure the most. Placing the moss ball in a spot with some good ventilation and shade is a good idea.

It is not impossible to raise moss balls indoors. You can leave moss balls by the window for weeks, as long as there is good lighting, and occasionally allow some contact with strong breezes. However, it is best to avoid an air conditioned room. The plant might not cope well with drastic and sudden changes in environment. You can bring the plant indoors to decorate your room during the day and take it out at night, or make similar accommodations, while monitoring its wellness.

Above left and above right Out on the porch, not placing the plants directly on the ground.
Right You may raise the moss balls indoors to a certain point, while being mindful of ventilation.

Watering

The basic way to give water is to submerge the moss ball, and once air bubbles stop coming out, you're done. You can use a watering can, but keep in mind that a watering can might not reach every nook and cranny, so be extra careful with this method. That said, you want to avoid flooding the moss ball.

When it comes to water, it's important to consider compatibility of your moss and plant combination from the outset. The best combination consists of moss and plants with similar needs.

Managing in Summer and Winter

Depending on where you place your moss in summer, the amount of watering will differ. This should be done early in the morning or during sunset. If you water during high temperatures, a lot of the water will evaporate and create a steamy environment, and this could possibly weaken the moss and plant.

Snow and freezing temperatures aren't a real problem for moss, but it could be a problem for the plant, so it is best to avoid placing the moss ball in a very cold spot. During winter, you just need to water the moss ball when the soil is dry.

No Need for Fertilizer

At a certain level, moss can survive by just having light and water, so there's no need for fertilizer. Fertilizer could actually be harmful to moss. Since we're not aiming to enlarge the roots, the plants basically don't need fertilizer either. If you want to give your plant some boost, you can add a very minimal amount of liquid fertilizer.

Even if it Looks Like it's Wilting...

When growing moss balls, you will surely encounter your plants wilting at some point. Don't give up when you see that happening. A plant might not adapt well to its new environment, which could cause discoloration. Once the plant adapts to its new home, new leaves will sprout, and your hard work will be rewarded. So give your moss ball some time, and take good care of it, and you will see great results.

When submerging the moss ball in water, air bubbles will come out. Make sure to not steep leaves or flowers in the water.

Mizugoke helps maintain humidity. This moss can take in a lot of water, and retain moisture.

A Japanese Pepper plant that lost all its leaves has grown new ones.

Moss Ball Q & A

Q: Any pests or disease we need to worry about?

A: Moss by comparison is resilient to diseases, so there isn't much to worry about. However, moss has a risk of moldering, so it is best to not overwater.

Q: My moss has gotten moldy. What should I do?

A: During the rainy or humid season, if you leave your moss ball in a place where there's no ventilation, or in a place with high humidity, mold is bound to appear. To counter this, you can rinse the moldy parts with water and use some tissue to gently take off the mold. Leave the moss ball in a well-ventilated place, and it should be OK. The mold will naturally dissipate.

Q: What kind of string should we use for the moss ball?

A: The color should be black or dark green, something that would not stand out. Cotton is fine, but after a while, the string might break, and the moss ball might fall apart. A sturdy nylon string could last longer.

Q: Should my moss turn red?

A: In general, moss doesn't change color. Even in winter, most moss remains green. When the moss dries up, it turns white or brown.

Q: The plant I used in my moss ball is still pretty young and small. What should I do when it gets bigger?

A: You can control growth by the amount of soil you use. Your plant should overgrow the moss ball. Roots that start coming out of the moss ball can be put back into the soil, or can just naturally wilt away. A plant with stems underground like Sasa (broadleaf bamboo), could possibly extend its parts to a neighboring moss ball. You could make a group (try to shape it upwards) or you can also just cut it off the extending parts.

Q: There are little needles sprouting out of my moss ball. What is this?

A: It's called sporophyte. The thick part is called moss sporangium (refer to p. 56).

Below left Sasa underground stem extending out. **Below middle** Katsura roots growing out of the soil, but that have been tucked back in.
Right Sporophyte sprouting.

Q : What is the life expectancy of the moss ball?

A : If the moss ball is raised in good conditions, it can live a good three years. When the moss gets old, or the plant doesn't seem to be doing well, you could always change the soil, or renew the moss. When it reaches its end you can just plant the whole ball in the ground.

Q : Is there a moss that shouldn't be used to make a moss ball?

A : Large moss such as Sugigoke isn't suitable to make moss balls. Moss that doesn't stick together well, also would be hard to handle. It is fun to experiment with different kinds of moss, but for starters, its a good idea to stick with simple mosses (refer to p. 16).

Sugigoke is a large moss, more suitable for outdoor gardening.

Q : No many how many moss balls I make, I always have one spot that dies off. Why does this happen?

A : It's possible that the soil that came with your plant had some fertilizer in it. The fertilizer could be causing the some of your moss to die. As mentioned in the care section of the book, moss doesn't mix well with fertilizer. This is why you would want to clear out as much of the original soil as much as possible.

Q : Can you make Goblin's Gold moss into a moss ball?

A : Using Goblin's Gold moss (*Schistostega*) alone or with luminescent plants in a moss ball sounds like a something out of a fantasy. Realistically speaking, it is difficult to use for a moss ball. Goblin's Gold moss is rare and isn't usually used in gardening, and to begin with it isn't suitable to make into a ball. It might be best to admire the fantasy-like moss in it's original habitat, and stick to mosses that are suitable to gardening.

Q : When I was making a moss ball, I ended up with leftover moss. What should I do?

A : There are ways to preserve the moss so you can use it for your next project. Here are a couple of tips to keep your moss green: ① Keep the moss moist. ② Keep moss in shade to partial shade, no direct sunlight. In order to keep the moss moist, keep in tight container or in a spot without too much air passage, so the moss doesn't dry out.

Haigoke being preserved out on the porch. This is the tray in it came in, covered with a mesh cloth to let some light through. The bottom is covered with plastic to keep moss from drying out.

Have Fun with Moss Orbs!

A moss orb is just moss wrapped around a ball of soil, held together with a string. The steps in making a moss orb are pretty much the same as for making a full-on moss ball.

The main difference is that without the addition of a plant, caring for a moss orb is much easier. Moss orbs are a great way to try out and learn the characteristics of different types of moss.

Hosobaokinagoke
Leucobryum juniperoideum

This is a gapless bundle of moss. It is neat and simple-looking. Best to always keep moist, and keep in indirect sunlight.

Haigoke
Hypnum plumaeforme

Wrap this ball in between leaves, to allow the leaves to grow into its natural shape. It has a mat-like quality, so it is easy to work with. Keep moist, and keep in indirect sunlight.

Hosourigoke
Brachymenium exile (Dozy et Molk.)

This is the moss you often see growing between the cracks of concrete. The secret to making this into a packed bundle lies in the way you get the bits to adhere together. Keep moist, and keep in indirect sunlight.

Brachythecium
Family *Brachytheciaceae*

This moss can be found on rocks, bark, and soil. It has a rather matte texture, is easy to deal with, but after about a month it sprouts weeds (as shown below). Keep moist, and keep in indirect sunlight.

Bryum
Family *Bryaceae*

Just like Hosobaokinagoke, this is a gapless bunch of moss. Keep moist, and keep in indirect sunlight. The image below is 5 months after assembled.

Thuidium
Family *Thuidiaceae*

The delicate detail of the leaves gives a calming feel. This is also a mat-like moss, which makes it easy to put together. This moss is really weak to dryness, so spread some Mizugoke at the bottom to help keep moist at all times (refer to p. 25). Keep in brighter shades.

★ **Mosses introduced in p. 28–30 are the most common mosses used in Japanese gardening.**

Hinokigoke *Pyrrhobryum dozyanum*

Also called Japanese Cypress. The leaves of this moss are bushy and soft. The moss has a large body mass, so gather each bundle together and wrap firmly to keep in place. Keep in partial shade, and water by misting heavily. This might be a tough one to raise.

Sunagoke *Racomitrium canescens*

It is also called Hoary Fringe-moss. This moss crumbles apart easily, so raising this moss might be difficult. Wrap string around this orb a good 5–6 times. If you spray to give water, it will grow leaves that bloom like flowers. Spray to give water, and keep in indirect sunlight.

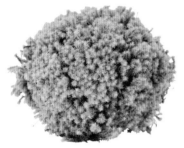

Kotsubogoke *Plagiomnium acutum*

Its smallness and roundness makes this moss cute. This can be kept together well with mindful wrapping. Keep moist, and keep in brighter shades.

Apple Moss *Bartramiaceae*

The pearls growing out of this moss will capture your heart. It's relatively difficult to make this into a ball, so it might require a lot of binding. It loves high humidity and a lot of light, but still requires shade. Spray to water. This one might be tough for beginners.

Mizugoke Sphagnum moss

Make from dry moss (image below), and add water while keeping in the shade. After you leave it for a while, you will get a green moss orb like the one on the right.

Silvery Bryum *Bryum argenteum*

Another moss you often see on the streets. While this moss grows in groups, it is somehow unexpectedly hard to keep together as a ball. Keep under indirect sunlight, and be careful to not overwater.

The Different Shapes of Moss Ball Gardens

Moss ball gardening doesn't restrict you to the spherical form. You can make other shapes, like a donut, or cylinder. Take up the challenge on some of these shapes.

When arranging the roots and soil, you form the different shapes. You just have to bind the moss with string to the soil. There's lots of fun you can have with this.

Yamagoke and Haigoke (the hair portion) shaped into a doll. There's a mix of moss on the head portion.

Haigoke and Hazelnut form an archway. With just a little bit of tweaking, you get an alternative style of moss gardening.

Haigoke and Hazelnut again, shaped into a donut. This couldn't really be called a moss ball—could it?

Haigoke and Rubus shaped into a cylinder, like a vase.

Growing a Chestnut in a Moss Ball

When you see chestnuts that have fallen from a tree, don't you feel like picking them up and doing something with them? Find a newly dropped chestnut in the fall, and plant it in your moss ball. This way your chestnut has a good chance of sprouting by springtime. But that doesn't mean you can't try planting the springtime nuts. We will show you how to raise nuts you picked in spring.

Left Stem sprouting out of planted chestnut. The root is steadily contained in the moss ball. Leave outside in the shade. You don't really need to worry about how big it will get. Surprisingly, it doesn't grow beyond the bounds of the moss ball it's planted in.

How to Raise a Chestnut

1. There are many kinds of chestnuts out there. Gather as many as you can, avoiding the ones with holes.

2. Leave in water overnight. Discard the ones that float—those have likely been hollowed out by insects.

3. Place the nuts with moistened Mizugoke in a container and close the lid. To increase the chances of sprouting, place in low temperatures. Keep in the refrigerator for three weeks or so.

4. The first one to sprout amongst our batch was the Japanese (Kunigi) chestnut.

5. The first sprout can finally be planted in the moss ball. You can even just place it in halfway.

6. About a month later, the stem starts to grow. It takes a while for the stem to sprout, but once the stem grows out enough, the growth accelerates.

7. After a couple of weeks, the leaves pop out. The fresh green leaves will take you by surprise. The moss ball may dry out faster at this stage, and needs water daily.

Other Chestnuts from the Batch is Sprouting!

After a month, some of the other nuts start to pop out some roots and stems.

Once the stem grows out a bit, plant the nut in the moss ball. You may get leaves within 2 weeks.

Fun with Dividing (Cloning)

When the plants in your moss ball begin to wilt, you can take out healthy parts to replant. Instead of taking your moss ball apart, you can cut and divide the stems to replant.

 Start How to Divide in 7 Steps

1. Cherry Sage is one plant that is easy to divide. Cut this off from the moss ball.

2. Cut off flowers and buds with scissors.

3. Cut out the young tips. Cut in angles.

4. Soak the tips you plan to use in water for around an hour.

5. Cut off any leaves at the bottom.

6. Insert stems into the moss ball.
7. While the stems are growing roots, keep in indirect sunlight and away from strong wind or rain. Make sure it doesn't dry up.

\ And it's done! /

Part 2

Enjoying
Moss

Where Can You Find Moss in Nature?

Of course you can see moss around town—in parks, peeking through cracks in concrete, and in other places. But if you're really interested in moss, you might want to take a look at some moss-rich areas. Here are a few recommendations for you.

First of all, mountain streams in forest trails. These areas make a pleasant environment for moss: water is flowing, the humidity is just right, and sunlight is shining through in just the right amount. The shapes of the mosses here are different from the ones you see in towns. It might be easier to distinguish and identify mosses out here because they are bigger in size.

If you take a look at rocks, or piles of stones around trees, you might notice all kinds of moss and spores growing. It is kind of rare to see many types of moss in town.

With the sounds of the leaves rustling, the river flowing, birds chirping, a walk in nature is a good stress reliever. The sound and smell of moss is a part of that. There is healing power in moss.

1. Moss-covered tree bridge along the stream.
2. Moss growing by the shore. 3. Stone table on the trail, being taken over by moss. 4. There are many kinds of moss growing on this big stone. 5. A moss-covered rock found in the river. It takes some time to get to this stage.

Moss Balls that Appear in Nature

This is the Oirase Gorge in Aomori Prefecture, Japan. You can see a variety of mosses growing on the rocks in the river. This is pretty much a naturally-formed moss ball. It is thought that seeds fell on the rock and plants simply sprouted. This stream is flowing from the Towada Lake, however, even when it rains the water rarely rises, so plants are able to live on moss rocks.

In the Woods and Forest

We tend to assume that since moss can live as long as there's light and water, the forest is sure to be covered in moss, but that's not true of all the forest's surfaces. Grasses and fallen leaves prevent sunlight from reaching the forest floor, making those areas unfriendly to moss growth. Even so, you'll notice that on fallen trees and their stumps, moss is growing.

You can see many kinds of moss in the rocky forests created by volcanic activity. Such a spot is the Shirakoma Pond in Nagano Prefecture, known as the "Moss Forest."★

Mt.Fuji harbors a hidden moss spot. It is registered as a World Cultural Heritage Site. There are plenty of mosses here because of the abundance of rain.

While Japan is at the forefront of interest in visiting mossy places, mosses certainly abound in other parts of the world, such as Olympic National Park in Washington (US), Banf National Park in Alberta (CA), Connemara National Park in Galway (IR) and indeed, in national forests around the world, wherever rainfall is plentiful. Wherever you go to see moss, try to view it up close.

★ Locations such as this one have been designated as "Japanese Protected Moss Forests."

1. Moss tightly clinging to a fallen tree. Plants are growing from the mossy trunk. 2. Hinokigoke growing on slopes of cedar trails. 3. Mossy forest grounds around the Shikakoma Pond. These are trees growing on moss rocks. 4. Fijino Mannengusa often seen around Mt. Fuji. 5. Moss growing in spots around tree trunks.

1. Moss growing on tree roots that grew by a small river. 2. Moss on concrete wall. 3. Haigoke growing where sunlight hits. Where sunlight reaches it grows well, but it looks a little brown. 4. Sunagoke growing on sand near fields.

Old Developed Landscapes

Landscapes where there was human activity is perfect for moss growth. The place was developed just for growing plants, so the amount of sunlight and soil should be just right. Overgrown areas with stone walls become a favorite place for moss.

1. Moss growing on top of a stone lantern. 2. Moss on spots where rainwater flows from a shrine roof. 3. Silvery bryum growing on a group of rocks. 4. Hosourigoke growing between the cracks of concrete bricks.

Shrines, Temples, Gardens

Well-kept gardens and temple landscapes intentionally emphasize moss growth. Some places are famous for their moss gardens, such as the Saihoji Temple in Kyoto, and the Hakone Museum of Art in Kanagawa Prefecture. You can generally see moss growing in shrines and temples, often in spots where rain drips down from copper roofs. It's said that copper ions are harmless, thus the moss that grows on it (Honomjigoke) goes by the common name Tongue-leaf copper moss.

In the City

Concrete-dominated urban areas can be a harsh environment for moss. Mosses such as Silvery bryum and Hosori are able to thrive by clumping together in small groups, allowing them to lose less moisture. Some cities deliberately cultivate moss to improve air quality.

Observing Moss

Start out by looking with the naked eye. While it is important to learn the name, the habitat, and the shape of the moss, first just get a feel for the moss itself. Get a general sense of the atmosphere of its living space. If you'd like to touch the moss, try gently stroking it. A basic tool for observing moss in detail is the magnifying glass. Place the lens close to the moss, and your eyes fairly close to the lens. Little spray bottles are also helpful to moisten dried up moss. When you wet the moss, the leaves will open up. Also, for good note-taking, you'll want a camera. A compact digital camera is a convenient choice. We recommend any kind that can take close-ups. A tripod is good for stability where there is low light.

Bottom You can get a great glimpse into the world of moss by looking through a magnifying glass. Here, you can see the leaves of Sugigoke.

Feel free to touch the carpet-like mosses.

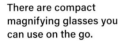

There are compact magnifying glasses you can use on the go.

A flip screen helps when taking photos at low angles.

A little spray bottle from the dollar store—easy to carry around.

You can use a scraper to collect moss from the ground or concrete cracks.

Keep moss safe in a closed plastic bag. When the moss starts to dry up, spray with some water. This way, the moss should be OK for a while. Keep away from direct sunlight.

During winter, moss that's on the ground may be pushed up and out by frost columns. This is when you can just collect by hand.

Collecting moss from protected areas is prohibited. (Check online for more information regarding your own local parks and trails.)

Collecting and Preserving Moss

You can see moss growing anywhere just outside your house. It is possible to just collect mosses near your home and play around with them.

You can use a scraper to collect colonies of moss. Remove any trash/debris that's on its surface. Preserve it by keeping it in a bag, leaving a little opening for air, and spritzing with water when needed. Always be aware of the quantities you are collecting, as over-collecting can disrupt the ecosystem. It takes a considerable amount of time for moss to grow back, so try to take as little as possible. Be aware that there are protected areas where any kind of collection is prohibited.

Terrariums

You can grow moss inside your room. The moss you've collected or purchased can be grown in a glass container like a terrarium. Anything from a flask to an old jar can do the job. Add to your home interior with different shapes of jars and kinds of mosses.

You can keep moss for quite a while in jars that have lids. Lids preserve moisture protect the moss from heavy air-conditioning. Jars without lids are actually easier for maintaining humidity, but it's still important to water properly and adequately.

Goldfish bowls and vases are also great. You can use them for moss orbs or keeping long-shaped mosses.

Combination of a few kinds of mosses.

Hosourigoke moss orb in a glass bowl.

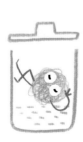

Try growing *Climacium japonicum* in a glass bowl. Thick layer of Fuji sand at the very bottom, then a thin layer of soil. On top of that there's Climacium, and laid with Thuidium. Climacium loves a lot of water, so on top of just spraying water, fill about 1–1½ inches (2–3 cm) of water from the bottom.

What You Need for a Terrarium

All containers should be washed thoroughly and sanitized. The bottom of the container should be layered with Fuji sand and/or fine pebbles to allow drainage thereby preventing root rot. A layer of activated charcoal can also facilitate drainage.

On top of that you can use one of the specially mixed terrarium soils, or any sanitized soil. This will be the base for the moss. Add moss onto the base, and if it seems to be falling over, just add more soil to fix it.

If you are using a container with a small neck, tweezers can be helpful. When laying the moss, make sure there aren't any gaps between the moss and the soil. Lightly spray to moisturize.

Daily Care

If you are keeping the moss in fairly narrow containers, or containers with lids, you basically don't have to do much. Two rules:
1) Do not leave in direct sunlight.
2) Do not give too much water.

Moss (Climacium)

Soil

Pebbles for drainage

Bark collected from the cedar woods. Any debris is removed from both sides. The bottom is layered with sand and soil, and some other mosses.

Left Moss on a bark and Climacium. **Center** Climacium. **Right** Hinokigoke and Hosourigoke.

When you keep containers in direct sunlight, the internal temperature can rise to the point where it will damage the moss. But beware the other extreme: don't keep it in a dark place. When the moss seems to be getting a little dry, spritz it, but careful to not overwater, as this will cause molding. If you think you've watered a little too much, leave the lid open for a while.

Bowl-shaped Containers

You can enjoy terrarium in glass bowls as well. Since it is without a lid, the care is no different from caring for moss balls. Kept outside the room, in the shade, and giving appropriate amounts of water when needed. When raising a moss orb inside a container, watering is the same as with moss balls—by soaking in water. However, if you have difficulty handing the orb, you can substitute soaking with heavy spraying.

Combination of tall Sugigoke and Bryum moss.

A rock is placed underneath the roots of Kotsubogoke.

Hosobaokinagoke terrarium. If you think you've overwatered, remove the lid for a while to let some water evaporate.

Propagating Moss

Moss grows from spores, but many mosses can be propagated using "cuttings." In Japan we call this process "Makigoke." Peel the moss with your hands, cut into small pieces with scissors, then evenly spread soil in a flowerpot. You can also use a transparent container with a lid for this process. For soil use akadama or black soil mixed with river sand.

Sprinkle a little soil on top to anchor the moss against breezes. It should be left in a place that's bright but not actually sunny. Spray to give moisture. About a month later, you might start seeing something green sprouting. However, depending on the conditions, you might not see any change even after three months. If you see no results, don't give up, as it may just be requiring more time. Smaller moss may grow faster than the larger ones. If you notice moss growing around your home, chances are your moss should be able to grow quickly.

Makigoke in a Container

Makigoke of Hosourigoke in a clear container with a lid attached (above). When shutting the lid, use a piece of paper or something to keep the lid from shutting completely (left).

After five months. Thin layer of green on the surface (above). Moss growing here and there (left).

Makigoke in Flowerpots

Makigoke of Hosourigoke in a small pot (right), then seven months later (far right). This is left outside, except when there is heavy wind or rain. After the long wait, some moss finally became visible.

This one is Silvery bryum. Tiny moss is showing after three months—it could be that it had adapted relatively quickly to its new home. Before you know it, you have new moss.

Combining Moss and Ferns

Attaching to a Tree Fern Pole

Fern and moss have similar habitats and cycles, so they make a good combination. For example, you can attach moss and fern to a Tree Fern pole (top image). Tree Fern comes in pots, poles, slabs and other shapes. This natural, woody fiber is porous and retains moisture well, and it's easy to cling to, so climbing plants really like it. Tree Fern is available in garden shops and online.

To attach, use some twine or wires to wrap the moss and fern to the trunk. Give plenty of water and keep in the shade. After some time, the fern and moss will become one with the trunk.

Fishing Line Moss Ball

Here, we've created a Shinobu moss ball with fern. Just as in creating any moss ball, we wrapped the moss around the ball of soil that holds the fern roots (refer to p. 92). You can also hang another moss ball to it (bottom right).

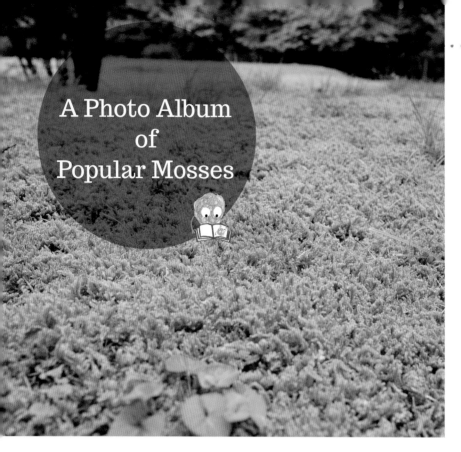

A Photo Album of Popular Mosses

Haigoke
Hypnum plumaeforme
Hypnaceae

This moss grows in colonies on straws or grass. Comparatively, it prefers brighter places. It's often yellow-green to yellow-brown in color. Some thick branches wing out regularly. This moss is often used in Zen gardening. It curls slightly when it dries up, but does not shrink excessively.

Hosobaokinagoke
Leucobryum juniperoideum
Dicranaceae

This moss tends to grow in round clumps on low lands, mountain lands, and around the bottom of tree trunks. It has a frosty green color. It loves the shade, and even when it dries up, the leaves don't change much. This moss is widely used in moss gardening. It could be called Arahashiragagoke or Yamagake. Arahashiragagoke is a large and leafy type.

Sunagoke
Racomitrium canescens
Grimmiaceae

Also called Hoary Fringe-moss. Grows in areas of good light, on sand or stones. It has a bright yellow-green color. The stem can grow up to 1 inch (3 cm) and contains a lot of leaves. When the moss dries up, the leaves shrink to the stem. When moisture is restored, the leaves immediately open back up. Used in moss gardening and to add greeness to buildings.

Thuidium
Thuidiaceae

Under shade, this moss grows in large groups on the ground or on stone. The stem is yellow and the branches wing out in pairs. The moss can grow large up to 8 inches (20 cm) at the stem. It has beautiful green leaves and a delicate shape. This is a great moss to use for moss balls and terrariums. (This genus includes the mosses known as Fern moss, Log moss and Mountain moss, among others).

Hinokigoke
Pyrrhobryum dozyanum
Rhizogoniaceae

Also called Japanese Cypress, this is a large type of moss that grows on humus in the mountain forests. You can see this in humid and partially-shaded places, such as along a valley. It is also known as "Itachi-noshippo" because of its soft bristles. Often used for gardening and terrariums.

Sugigoke
Polytrichaceae

Also called Hair Cap Moss. You can see this moss from lowlands to humus on mountain grounds. It looks similar to cedar. When dried up the leaves close up to the stem. This moss has various types, some of which as are tall as 8 inches (20 cm) long and others as short as 1–1½ inches (2–3 cm) long. Often used in moss gardening.

Apple Moss
Bartramiaceae

Usually grown in lumps on wet grounds, rocks, and mountain cliffs. It prefers partially-shaded areas. The leaves are thin and sharp, and shrink when they're dried up. You can see charming spheres sprouting during the spring.

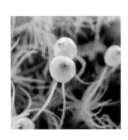

Climacium
Climaciaceae

This large moss can be found in humus in the mountain forests and can be found growing by rivers. Half of the stem is in the soil and grows many branches, rather like a tree. It is similar to other mosses such as Furousou and Fujinomannen-gusa. Furousou is not so tall, and grows upright. Fujinomannengusa has many small branches at the top. Often used for gardening and terrariums.

Kotsubogoke
Plagiomnium acutum
Mniaceae

From residential areas to foohills, in the shaded areas you'll see this moss growing on the ground or stones. It can grow both upright and outward. The egg-shaped leaves grow out in two rows. The rhizoid comes out to help new stems grow.

Mizugoke
Sphagnum moss
Sphagnaceae

This moss can be seen growing on humus and in wetlands. It is often used in gardening to insulate and help the soil retain moisture, and has uses outside of gardening as well.

Silvery Bryum
Bryaceae

This moss is quite popular. It can be seen in many places, bright shade to shaded areas, in gardens or concreted areas. It is relatively persistent to dryness. The tips of the leaves have a grayish-white color. Often used in bonsai and moss gardening.

Hyophila Moss
Pottiaceae

You can often see this moss in sunny places and under the shade, growing on concrete walls and stone surfaces. It has a green to brown color. It has a radial growing pattern, so the leaves curl up in a spiral.

Hosourigoke
Brachymenium exile (Dozy et Molk.)
Bryaceae

You can see this bluish moss growing in colonies between the cracks of concrete and stone steps. Sometimes this moss is grown with silvery bryum, as its look is similar. When given moisture, the leaves open up.

Honmonjigoke
Scopelophila cataractae
Pottiaceae

Also called Tongue-leaf Copper Moss. The name of this moss derived from the Ikegami Honmon-ji Temple in Tokyo, which is where it was first discovered in Japan. It is often found in places where rainwater falls or flows through, such as on top of copper roofs. It is found more in urban areas than in the mountains.

Brachythecium Moss
Brachytheciaceae

This moss often grows in shaded areas at a tree's roots or on the ground surrounding them. It isn't unusual to find this in urban areas. The stems crawl to the side and eventually form a carpet.

Bryum Moss
Bryaceae

In shaded areas, this moss is usually seen on concrete, flowerpots, tree trunks or rocks. Usually found in towns. When dried up, the leaves will curl up in a spiral. There are about 25 species of Bryum moss in Japan.

Shippogoke
Dicranium howellii
Dicranaceae

This moss grows in colonies, on top of humus in the forest or at tree roots. When dried up, the leaves tend to bend in the same direction. There are about 20 species in Japan.

Tachigoke
Atrichum undulatum
Polytrichaceae

Also called Common Smoothcap moss In shaded areas from lowland to mountains, this moss grows on wet soil or stones. It seems to be softer than Sugigoke, and the leaves are about ¼ inch (7–8 mm) long. The leaves shrink when dried up. This moss is also often used in gardening.

Iwadaregoke
Hylocomium splendens (Hedw.) Schimp.
Hylocomiaceae

This moss is found in the shaded areas in the forests. They grow in large colonies on humid soils, such as humus or on rocks. The new stem grows upward from the middle of the previous stem, which creates stair steps. Long ones may grow over 8 inches (20 cm).

Houougoke
Fissidens dubius
Fissidens

This moss lives on partially-shaded grounds or on wet rocks near the mountain stream. The pairs of leaves grow thick. It takes its name from its appearance of the leaves, which resemple the tail of a cocoon. About 42 different kinds of this moss can be found in Japan.

Goblin's Gold Moss
Schistostega pennata
Schistostegaceae

Also called Dragon's Gold. This moss grows in dim and damp places such as in mountain caves, or gaps between rocks. The stem is about ¼ inch (7–8 mm) long, and the leaves grow in two rows, one on each side of the stem. It's not the leaves or stems that cause the moss to glow. Cells of the "protomata" germinate from spores, and before they take plant form, their spherical cells act as lenses that absorb and reflect light. The glow can been seen in very dim light only.

Moss Ecology

How to Preserve Moisture

Unlike most other plants, moss has no real roots to absorb water or nutrients. The only thing supporting the body is the rhizoid. Moss absorbs water from the leaves and stems. Without moisture, photosynthesis stops, preventing growth. Therefore, mosses gather in a colony, forming in ways that help preserve moisture.

Surviving Dehydration

Even if the moss dries up, it doesn't immediately die out. For most kinds of moss, once they receive moisture they usually revive. The leaves just shrink or curl up when they are thirsty, waiting to come back to life.

There Are Several Ways to Multiply

Moss generally propagates via spores. After fertilization, the spore body extends upwards, and the tip is covered with spore-packed pods. Spores are released from these pods and are airborne. There are also other, more successful ways of propagating. For example, moss can multiply asexually. Loose or broken pieces of moss can travel by air and establish new growth where they land, if the conditions are right. Moss can also form new plants from broken stems and leaves. Some mosses are easy to separate, some stick to the back of animals, or shoes, and go on a journey to breed.

Why Isn't It Being Eaten? Does It Taste Bad?

Compared to other plants, mosses are rarely eaten by animals or insects. That might be because the moss looks unappetizing, a natural defense mechanism. In addition, they are said to have antibacterial properties that protect them from rotting easily or growing mold.

Please note

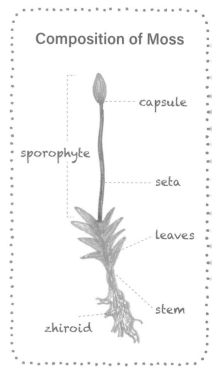

Dried up Sugigoke (left), and watered Sugigoke (right).

Composition of Moss

capsule

sporophyte

seta

leaves

stem

zhiroid

Zenigoke can often be spotted in the shaded areas of the garden.

Mosses, Liverworts and Hornworts

Generally, the plant type commonly referred to as "moss" are actually Bryophytes, of which moss is simply one type. The leaves of mosses are simple and their texture is generally velvety. Within this group there are upright types such as the the Sugigoke (Common Haircap moss), and creeping types such as the Haigoke. Most bryophytes used in gardening are mosses. Liverworts' leaves are lobed in shape. The Zenigoke is an example of a liverwort. Hornworts are similar to liverworts, but their leaves are more irregular in shape. There are far fewer known species of hornworts than of mosses or liverworts.

Part 3

100
Moss Balls
to Try

★ For detailed information on soils used for moss balls, refer to p. 17. The basic watering guideline for winter is to water when the moss ball becomes dry and lightweight.

Flowering Plant Moss Balls

Cherry Blossom
Rosaceae, Prunus (Deciduous Tall Tree)

Cherry Blossom or Sakura is the emblem of Japan. Whether it is used in bonsai or planted in a flower-pot, it can be enjoyed as a small plant. There are many varieties, such as Gotemba Sakura, Asahisakura, and so on. Some varieties bloom early, so you might want to do some preliminary research before you choose. If you make a moss ball while the plant is growing buds, you can look forward to seeing the flowers bloom. Single-flowering types will wilt quickly, but double-flowering plants allow you to enjoy the flowers a little longer.

SOIL Soil with good drainage **LIGHTING** Plenty of light and air circulation. Keep in partial shade during summer. **BLOOMING** March to April **WATERING** Once daily. Do not neglect watering especially before and after blooming. **DIFFICULTY** Average

Cherry Blossom is double-flowered. The base plant will have flowers blooming in May-June.

Yamabuki
Rosaceae, Kerria (Deciduous shrub)

Yamabuki has long been a favorite shrub in Japan, known for its beautiful yellow flowers that blume in spring. Cultivars produce types with white flowers, double flowers, and other types. Prune it shortly after flowering.

SOIL Soil with good drainage **LIGHTING** Plenty of light and air circulation. Keep in partial shade during summer. **BLOOMING** March to June **WATERING** Once daily **DIFFICULTY** Easy

★ **Pictured here is the spotted variety.**

Bridal Wreath
Spiraea prunifolia
Rosaceae, Spiraea (Deciduous shrub)

A native of China. In spring it produces many double-flowered white blossoms. Often seen in parks and gardens around the world. Reeve's Spiraea and Yukiyanagi are part of the same group. The branches can get a little wild, so try to keep neatly trimmed.

SOIL Soil with good drainage **LIGHTING** Plenty of light and air circulation. Keep in partial shade during summer. **BLOOMING** April to May **WATERING** When the moss ball becomes light, add plenty of water. **DIFFICULTY** Easy

Azalea

▶ Ericaceae, Rhododendron (Evergreen/ Deciduous shrub)

Often used in home gardening for its vivid flower colors. Satsuki Azalea is a popular type of Rhododenron. When pruning in fall and winter, be careful to not trim the branches too much.

SOIL Soil with good drainage. Slight acidity is preferred, so peat moss may be mixed in the soil. **LIGHTING** Plenty of light and air circulation. Keep in partial shade during summer. **BLOOMING** April to May **WATERING** Water generously once daily. **DIFFICULTY** Easy

★ **Pictured here is a Satsuki Azalea.**

Plum Blossom

◀ Rosaceae, Chaenomales (Deciduous shrub)

The plant now called the Plum Blossom or Ume was originally called the Kusaboke. It blooms red and white flowers. It is popular as a bonsai, and is associated with good fortune. Recommended for beginners as it's very resilient to both hot and cold weather.

SOIL Soil with good drainage **LIGHTING** Plenty of light and air circulation. Keep in partial shade during summer. **BLOOMING** Possible year-round **WATERING** Water generously once daily. **DIFFICULTY** Easy

White Ume

Hinasou

Houstonia caerulea L.

▶ Rubiaceae, Houstonia (Perennial plant)

Native to North America, nicknamed Quaker Ladies. There are blue and white flower varieties, and the flowers produced are plentiful. Adding some grass type of plant can be a good mash-up.

SOIL Soil with good drainage **LIGHTING** Plenty of light and air circulation. Keep in partial shade during summer. **BLOOMING** March to May **WATERING** When the moss ball becomes light, add plenty of water. **DIFFICULTY** Easy

Bridal Wreath

Reeve's spiraea

◀ Rosaceae, Spiraea (Deciduous shrub)

Native to China. The white flowers bloom in a sphere. The cluster-filled branches are its unique trait. There are double-flowered types, and spotted ones as well. They are easy to grow and very hardy.

SOIL Soil with good drainage **LIGHTING** Plenty of light and air circulation. Keep in partial shade during summer. **BLOOMING** April to May **WATERING** Water generously once daily. **DIFFICULTY** Easy

Hime Lilac

▶ Oleaceae, Syringa reticulata (Deciduous shrub)

A lilac native to China. Smaller than most lilacs, and so suitable to container planting. The flower has a pleasant scent. Prune after flowering is done.

SOIL Soil with good drainage **LIGHTING** Plenty of light and air circulation. Keep in partial shade during summer. **BLOOMING** April to May **WATERING** Water once daily **DIFFICULTY** Easy

Hime Lilac flower

Boronia

◀ Rutaceae, Boronia (Evergreen shrub)

Native to Australia. The leaves and flowers emit a refreshing citrus scent. Flower colors range from pale pink to a reddish brown. The *Boronia pinata*, pictured here, is generally light pink and can produce many flowers. The flower lasts relatively long.

SOIL Soil with good drainage **LIGHTING** Prefers partial shade. **BLOOMING** March to April **WATERING** When moss ball becomes light add plenty of water. **DIFFICULTY** Easy

Lily of the Valley

▶ Liliaceae, Convallaria (Perennial plant)

Lily of the Valley is loved in many parts of the world. The Japanese type is distributed from the central region and Hokkaido. It produces fragrant white flowers, and when fall comes along, there will be orange berries. These are poisonous, so keep your plant away from children and pets. When the leaves die in fall, they tend to remain on the stem, so be sure to cut them off at the base. Rather than combining with other plants, it is best to enjoy it on its own.

SOIL Soil with good drainage **LIGHTING** Plenty of light and air circulation. Keep in partial shade during summer. **BLOOMING** March to April **WATERING** Water once daily **DIFFICULTY** Average

★ **Pictured is the common *Convallaria majalis*.**

Columbine

◀ Ranunculaceae, Aquilegia (Perennial plant)

Widely distributed in the Northern Hemisphere and produces beautiful drooping flowers. Dwarf varieties are good for including in moss balls. Most regular Japanese varieties are smaller than Western types and so are also suitable for moss balls. During winter, the top portion wilts, so you may want to pair this up with an evergreen.

SOIL Soil with good drainage **LIGHTING** Plenty of light and air circulation. Keep in partial shade during summer. **BLOOMING** March to June **WATERING** Water once daily. Be careful not to give too much. **DIFFICULTY** Average

★ **In Japanese this flower is called the Furin Odamaki. It's chief characteristic is the bell shape of its flowers.**

Sekkoku

Dendrobia moniliforme

▶ Orchidaceae, Dendrobium (Perennial plant)

Distributed in Japan, China, and throughout the Korean Peninsula. The flower grows out straight from the stem. The colors of the flowers differ according to the variety. The flowers have a lovely subtle fragrance.

SOIL Soil with good drainage **LIGHTING** Plenty of light and air circulation. Keep in partial shade during summer. **BLOOMING** May to June **WATERING** Once the moss ball becomes light, add water. When the moss dries up, spray to hydrate. **DIFFICULTY** Average

Paper Cascade
◀ Asteraceae, Helipterum (Perennial plant)

These are of Mediterranean origin. The flower bud is pink, but when it blooms the flower turns white. The flower blooms for a long time. It can be dried and made into potpourri. When it overgrows, you can prune it wherever there's excess growth. Be careful to not overwater.

SOIL Soil with good drainage LIGHTING Plenty of light and air circulation. Keep in partial shade during summer. BLOOMING March to July WATERING Once the moss ball becomes light, add water. DIFFICULTY Average

Cattleya Clover
▶ Fabaceae, Trifolium (Perennial plant)

Broadly European. It is smaller than the average clover variety. You can admire the purple flowers starting from spring. There will be less foliage during the summer but it will grow back out during fall. Be careful not to give too much water.

SOIL Soil with good drainage LIGHTING Plenty of light and air circulation. Keep in partial shade during summer. BLOOMING March to July WATERING Once daily DIFFICULTY Easy

Mini Rose
◀ Rasaceae, Rosa (Deciduous shrub)

Native to the Northern Hemisphere. There are different types to choose from, with many different colors. They are easy to grow and they bloom each year. After flowering, pruning is required. Cut off at the top group of five leaves to allow the next flower to bloom.

SOIL Soil mixed with 30% to 40% peat moss LIGHTING Plenty of light and air circulation. Keep in partial shade during summer. BLOOMING Spring to fall WATERING When the moss ball becomes light, add water. DIFFICULTY Average

Lady Banks' moss ball. It has no thorns and is easy to handle. Its care can be the same as for the mini rose.

Clubmoss Mountain Heather
▶ Ericaceae, Cassiope (Perennial plant)

Grows in rocky highlands. This plant has thin, beard-like leaves, and small bell-shaped white flowers. There are varieties grown in Europe that have smaller flowers than this variety produces. The plant is weak to high temperatures and humidity.

SOIL Soil with good drainage **LIGHTING** Plenty of light and air circulation. Keep in partial shade during summer. **BLOOMING** April to May **WATERING** When the moss ball becomes light, add water. **DIFFICULTY** Average

★ **Pictured here is the *Cassiope lycopodioides* 'Beatrice Lilley'.**

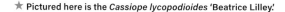

Kumomagusa
Western type
◀ Saxifragaceae, Saxifraga (Perennial plant)

Grows in rocky highlands. It has adorable little flowers. Dislikes excessive heat and it's best to avoid rain. Hibernates during winter.

SOIL Soil with good drainage **LIGHTING** Plenty of light and air circulation. Keep in partial shade during summer. **BLOOMING** March to May **WATERING** When the moss ball becomes light, add water. When watering make sure the water doesn't touch the flowers and leaves. **DIFFICULTY** Difficult

Iwachidori
▶ Orchidaceae, Ponerorchis (Perennial plant)

This grows in the central region of Japan, thriving in rocky areas. The flowers are tiny sweet blossoms of purple, pink or white, and grow out straight from the tip of the stem.

SOIL Soil with good drainage **LIGHTING** Plenty of light and air circulation. Keep in partial shade during summer. **BLOOMING** April to May **WATERING** Once daily Make sure water doesn't collect on the leaves. Place in a dish with wet mizugoke to keep constantly moist. **DIFFICULTY** Average

Jeffersonia Dubia
◀ Berberidaceae, Jeffersonia (Perennial plant)

A mountain grass that naturally grows in China and the Korean Peninsula. After the sweet purple flowers bloom, the leaves will grow (refer to p. 22). During winter the top part disappears, and reappears during spring.

SOIL Soil with good drainage **LIGHTING** Plenty of light and air circulation. Keep in partial shade during summer. **BLOOMING** April to May **WATERING** Water generously once daily. **DIFFICULTY** Quite Difficult

Doubling Larch
◀ Ranunculaceae, Thalictrum (Perennial plant)

Native to North America. It is a popular wildflower with small flowers. It is resistant to drying, and comes in any varieties including types with double flowers, or white and yellow-green flowers. It will hibernate from fall to spring. When combining with others, try using plants that grow beneath trees.

SOIL Soil with good drainage **LIGHTING** Plenty of light and air circulation. Keep in partial shade during summer. **BLOOMING** April to May **WATERING** Water generously once daily. **DIFFICULTY** Average

Wildowsill Orchid
Taiwanese Pleione or Pleione formosana
▶ Orchidaceae, Pleione (Perennial plant)

An orchid native to the Taiwanese highlands. To help ensure blooming for the following year, keep in a well-lit place so the stem will grow large and sturdy.

SOIL Soil with good drainage. Can also mixed with some mizugoke. **LIGHTING** Plenty of light and air circulation. Keep in partial shade during summer. **BLOOMING** April to May **WATERING** Water generously once daily. Make sure water doesn't collect in the leaves or stems. **DIFFICULTY** Average

Carnation
◀ Caryophyllaceae, Dianthus (Perennial plant)

Native to Europe and Asia. This flower features in many bouquets, but is also a lovely element in gardening, with many types to choose from. To prevent disease and pests, it should be diligently plucked. Be careful of excess moisture.

SOIL Soil with good drainage **LIGHTING** Plenty of light and air circulation. Keep in partial shade during summer. **BLOOMING** April to June **WATERING** When the moss ball becomes light, add plenty of water. **DIFFICULTY** Average

Eastern Blue-eyed Grass

Sisyrinchium rosulatum

▸ Iridaceae, Sisyrinchium (Perennial plant)

Native to North American grassland, this is called Niwazeki-shou in Japanese. The little purple flower grows out like a little iris. Combining with some grass plants is a good idea. Trim off the older leaves.

SOIL Soil with good drainage **LIGHTING** Plenty of light and air circulation. Keep in partial shade during summer. **BLOOMING** April to May **WATERING** Water generously once daily. **DIFFICULTY** Easy

The Elderflower

Violet

Viola mandshurica

◂ Violaceae, Viola (Perennial plant)

Called Sumire in Japanese, this is the wild flower that represents spring. The *Viola* genus is at home in many parts of the world, and there are many colors to choose from, from purple to yellow. It is a perennial plant, but after two or three years, the stock weakens.

SOIL Soil with good drainage **LIGHTING** Plenty of light and air circulation. Keep in partial shade during summer. **BLOOMING** March to May **WATERING** Water generously once daily. **DIFFICULTY** Average

Brassavola

▸ *Orchidaceae, Brassavola (Perennial plant)*

This orchid is native to Central and South America. It has long slender leaves, and multiple flowers that grow out of a single stem. During spring to fall, take care to ensure that it doesn't dry out.

SOIL Soil with good drainage **LIGHTING** Plenty of light and air circulation. Keep in partial shade during summer. **BLOOMING** Possible year-round **WATERING** Water generously once daily. **DIFFICULTY** Average

★ **This is the little stars variety.**

Oncidium

Chinese Ground Orchid

Asian Bleeding Heart

Oncidium
Orchidaceae, Oncidium
(Perennial plant)

This plant is a type of Orchid that native to Central and South America. It has a sweet yellow flower. It is looks very common, but there are many colors and type you can choose, which makes this plant fun to work with.

SOIL Soil with good drainage. Mizugoke is also good. **LIGHTING** Plenty of light and air circulation. Keep in partial shade during summer. **BLOOMING** Possible year-round **WATERING** Water generously once daily. **DIFFICULTY** Average

⭐ **This variety is called Oncidium 'Twinkle Orange Days' and puts out many lovely orange flowerets.**

Asian Bleeding Heart
Papaveraceae, Lamprocapnos
(Perennial plant)

Called Kemansou in Japan, this plant looks a little like fish hanging from a fishing rod. The heart-shaped flowers come in many colors. During fall, the leaves will wilt, fall and go dormant.

SOIL Soil with good drainage **LIGHTING** Plenty of light and air circulation. Keep in partial shade during summer. **BLOOMING** May to June **WATERING** Water generously once daily. **DIFFICULTY** Average

Chinese Ground Orchid
Orchidaceae, Bletilla
(Perennial plant)

Grows naturally in the wild in foothills. A light purple flower will bloom in early summer. There are many varieties, and it's a popular garden flower, as it's suitable to group planting. Trim the leaves when they turn red during fall and winter.

SOIL Soil with good drainage **LIGHTING** Plenty of light and air circulation. Keep in partial shade during summer. **BLOOMING** May to June **WATERING** When the moss ball becomes light, add plenty of water. **DIFFICULTY** Easy

Spotted Bellflower combined with the Balloon Flower and tall grass.

Iwayukinoshita
Hydrangea paniculata
Saxifragaceae, Saxifraga (Perennial plant)

Also called the Panicled Hydrangea. Can be seen growing along wetter areas such as the mountain streams. It is closely related to Daimonjisou and Yukinoshita, which have small white flowers. This plant should never be allowed to dry out.

SOIL Soil with good drainage **LIGHTING** Keep in half-shade to partial shade.**BLOOMING** May to June **WATERING** When the moss ball becomes light, add plenty of water. **DIFFICULTY** Average

Iwayukinoshita flower (right). Its close relative Yukinoshita. These require the same type of care.

Spotted Bellflower
Campanulaceae, Campanula (Perennial plant)

Grows along foot hills. During early summer, a drooping flower will bloom. There are many flower shapes and colors to choose from.

SOIL Soil with good drainage **LIGHTING** Plenty of light and air circulation. Keep in partial shade during summer. **BLOOMING** May to July **WATERING** When the moss ball becomes light, add plenty of water. **DIFFICULTY** Easy

Daimonjisou
Saxifraga fortunei var. Alpine
◀ Saxifragaceae, Saxifraga (Perennial plant)

This species is native to South Asia. Often seen along swampy areas. Flowers appear in the fall; white flowers are most common, but there are also red and pink varieties.

SOIL Soil with good drainage **LIGHTING** Keep in bright shaded areas **BLOOMING** September to November **WATERING** When the moss ball becomes light, add plenty of water. **DIFFICULTY** Average

Daimonjisou Flower

Combined with Tosamisuzu and Chidakesashi.

Mountain Hydrangea
Hydrangeaceae, Hydrangea
(Deciduous shrub)

There are many types of hydrangea, with their flowers varying in color and shape. After flowering, pruning is required. You can enhance the hydrangea's charm by combining with other plants. In Japan you can see this variety in many areas starting from Kanto to down south in Kyushu.

SOIL Soil with good drainage **LIGHTING** Plenty of air circulation. Keep in half-shade. **BLOOMING** May to July **WATERING** Water generously once daily. **DIFFICULTY** Easy

Combined with fern.

Starrish Whitetop

Rhynchospora colorata (Dichromena colorata)

▶ Cyperaceae, Rhynchospora (Perennial plant)

Native to North America, this plant grows in the wetlands. Its unique trait is the long stems, and flowers popping out of the tips like fireworks. This plant requires constant moisture, so be aware of the soil drying up. The top part will wilt away during winter, but the stem will grow back out during spring.

SOIL Soil with good drainage LIGHTING Plenty of light and air circulation. Keep in partial shade during summer. BLOOMING June to July WATERING Water generously once daily. You can keep wet mizugoke at the bottom of the plate for plenty of moisture. DIFFICULTY Easy

Right Combination with Corkscrew Rush and Longstyle Rush.

Dwarf Meadow Rue

Thalictrum kiusianum

◀ Ranunculaceae, Thalictrum (Perennial plant)

This mountain grass reaches about 4 inches (10 cm) in height. It's easy to work with, and is popular as ground cover. The flowers range from pinkish purple to lavender.

SOIL Soil with good drainage LIGHTING Plenty of light and air circulation. Keep in partial shade during summer. BLOOMING June to July WATERING Water generously once daily. DIFFICULTY Easy

Left Hime Bamboo is added behind the Shikushikara-matsum.

Suzukakesou

Veronicastrum villosulum
Plantaginaceae, Veronicastrum (Perennial plant)

A perennial plant native to China. The leaves grow out unevenly. As the plant grows out, a purple flower will eventually appear. You can leave it in a high place, and also use some kind of stake for support since it is a climber.

SOIL Soil with good drainage **LIGHTING** Plenty of light and air circulation. Keep in partial shade during summer. **BLOOMING** July to August **WATERING** Water generously once daily. **DIFFICULTY** Easy

Suzukakesou Flower

Chinese Spiranthes

Orchidaceae, Spiranthes (Perennial plant)

The *Spiranthes* genus is also known as Lady's Tresses. Different *Spirathes* can be found in different parts of the world, and depending on the variety, the stem inter-twines and the flowers grow in a spiral, giving the plant a quirkly appearance.

SOIL Soil with good drainage **LIGHTING** Plenty of light and air circulation. Keep in partial shade during summer. **BLOOMING** June to July **WATERING** When the moss ball become light, add water. **DIFFICULTY** Average

Chinese Spiranthes Flower

A bamboo skewer gives good support.

Set in a cage or cage-like container, the vine can trail downward through the bars.

Or, set the container on the ground, and let the vine creep along.

Morning Glory
Convolvulaceae, Ipomoea (Annual plant)

Morning glory was introduced to Japan during the Edo period. First cultivated from China for ornamental use, this flower has become a symbol of summer in Japan. There are many species and they can be found in many parts of the world. Flowers come in many sizes, shapes and colors. If you plant seeds early in May, the plant may grow large. If you delay planting until August, you can see mini leaves sprouting. For moss balls, the latter option is the better bet. You may want to plant the seeds in a pot first before putting into a moss ball. It is a climber, so you may want to support it with a stake.

SOIL Soil with good drainage **LIGHTING** Plenty of light and air circulation. Keep in partial shade during summer. **BLOOMING** July to September **WATERING** Water once daily. **DIFFICULTY** Easy

White Egret Flower

▶ Orchidceae, Pecteilis (Perennial plant)

This wetlands orchid is native to the Far East, and in that region it still grows in the wild, but is decreasing. It's loved for the feathery, wing-like flowers that give it its name. If you have the opportunity to seek them in the wild, check the leaves and stems for signs of bacterial spots before gathering.

SOIL Soil with good drainage **LIGHTING** Plenty of light and air circulation. Keep in partial shade during summer. **BLOOMING** July to August **WATERING** Water generously once daily. You can keep wet mizugoke at the bottom of the plate for plenty of moisture. **DIFFICULTY** Average

Balloon Flower

◀ Campanulaceae, Platycodon (Perennial plant)

Also called the Japanese Bellflower or the Chinese Bellflower. Widely distributed in East Asia, where it was once readily found in the wild, but is becoming rare. The star-shaped purple flower has been a longtime favorite in Japan. Double-flowered and other varieties are also available.

SOIL Soil with good drainage **LIGHTING** Plenty of light and air circulation. Keep in partial shade during summer. **BLOOMING** June to September **WATERING** Once per day, give plenty of water. **DIFFICULTY** Easy

Shichouge

Leptodermis pulchella Yatabe

▶ Rubiaceae, Leptodermis (Deciduous shrub)

This particular species is native to Japan but grows similarly to other speciecs of *Leptodermis*. Flowers grow at the end of the branch and have a long blooming period.

SOIL Soil with good drainage **LIGHTING** Plenty of light and air circulation. Keep in partial shade during summer. **BLOOMING** June to September **WATERING** When the moss ball becomes light, add water. **DIFFICULTY** Average

A closeup of the blossom.

Planted with a bit of Burning Bush in front.

Shiratamahoshikusa

Eriocaulon nudicuspe Maxim

Eriocaulaceae, Eriocaulon (Annual plant)

The genus *Eriocaulon*, commonly known as Pipewort, grows mainly in wetlands and includes species in many parts of the world. Its tiny flowers grow out at the end of slender stalks, which reach different heights. The flower is fairly hardy and can be enjoyed for a relatively long time.

SOIL Soil with good drainage. Prefers some acidity, so mixing with some peat moss is also a good idea **LIGHTING** Plenty of light and air circulation. Keep in partial shade during summer. **BLOOMING** July to September **WATERING** Water generously once daily. You can keep wet mizugoke at the bottom of the plate for plenty of moisture. **DIFFICULTY** Average

Red Spider Lily

Amaryllidaceae, Lycoris (Perennial plant)

These form colonies in fields and hills during fall. The red flowers grow out from thick, firm stems. When the flowering is over, dark green leaves appear, which are equally lovely (see p. 22). You can grow them either from bulbs or sprouted stocks. There are some gardening varieties, differing in color and shape.

SOIL Soil with good drainage **LIGHTING** Plenty of light and air circulation. Keep in partial shade during summer. **BLOOMING** June to September **WATERING** Water generously once daily. **DIFFICULTY** Easy

Bluebeard
Caryopteris incana
Lamiaceae, Caryoteris (Perennial plant)

This plant is called Dangiku (dark chrystanthemum) in Japan. It is widely distributed in East Asia, primarily in rocky areas. The little flowers encircle the stems. These plants can be seen with pink as well as with purple flowers.

SOIL Soil with good drainage **LIGHTING** Plenty of light and air circulation. Keep in partial shade during summer. **BLOOMING** August to October **WATERING** When the moss ball becomes light, add water. **DIFFICULTY** Easy

Combination with Yellow Star Jasmine and Bluebeard. The Bluebeard blooms between October to December.

Murechidori Flock of Birds
Orchidaceae, Stenoglottis (Perennial shrub)

This is a member of the Stenoglottis orchid species, and is native to Africa. You'll see plenty of flowers growing at the tip of the stem. It is quite vulnerable to the cold, so monitor closely when the temperature goes below 41ºF/5ºC.

SOIL Soil with good drainage **LIGHTING** Keep in half-shaded place **BLOOMING** September to October **WATERING** When the moss ball becomes light, add water. **DIFFICULTY** Average

Marsh Grass of Parnassus
Parnassia palustris
▶ Celastraceae, Parnassia (Perennial plant)

Can be seen in mountainous areas in the Northern Hemisphere. Its overall size is small. During summer you'll see white plum-like flowers blooming. This species has several varieties.

SOIL Soil with good drainage **LIGHTING** Keep in half-shaded place **BLOOMING** September to October **WATERING** When the moss ball becomes light, add water. **DIFFICULTY** Average

Right The one in the image is another type of Parnassus (Kamitsu), which is easy to handle.

Tamurasou
Serratula coronata subsp. *insularis*
◀ Asteraceae, Serratula (Perennial plant)

Can be seen along the mountain lands in Japan. The flowers bloom at the beginning of fall. This is a form of thistle, but this subspecies is thornless.

SOIL Soil with good drainage **LIGHTING** Keep in half-shaded place **BLOOMING** August to October **WATERING** When the moss ball becomes light, add water. **DIFFICULTY** Average

Left The type of Tamurasou in the image is a variation with more small detailed leaves.

Okera
Atractylodes japonica
▶ Asteraceae, Atractylodes (Perennial plant)

Native to Central East Asia. The flowers bloom during fall. At one time it was used for medicinal purposes. Make sure there is no excess moisture. There are also red and white flower varieties. A moss ball combining the two colors can be lovely.

SOIL Soil with good drainage **LIGHTING** Plenty of light and air circulation. Keep in partial shade during summer. **BLOOMING** September to October **WATERING** When the moss ball becomes light, add water. **DIFFICULTY** Easy

Right Combining with fern or Red Okera gives it a elegant touch.

Iwashajin

Adenophora takedae

▶ Campanulaceae, Adenophora (Perennial plant)

This bellflower species is native to Japan and can be seen growing in the rocky areas in the Kanto and Chubu. It grows drooping light purple flowers, which looks very delicate. It shines during the fall season. Be careful of excess moisture.

SOIL Soil with good drainage **LIGHTING** Plenty of light and air circulation. Keep in partial shade during summer. **BLOOMING** September to October **WATERING** When the moss ball becomes light, add water. **DIFFICULTY** Average

Fujibakama

Eupatorium japonicum

◀ Asteraceae, Eupatorium (Perennial plant)

A wild flower growing along Japan's Kanto to Kansai regions. Grayish-purple flowers bloom in the fall. Many *Eupatorium* species are native to North America.

SOIL Soil with good drainage **LIGHTING** Plenty of light and air circulation. Keep in partial shade during summer. **BLOOMING** September to October **WATERING** Once per day **DIFFICULTY** Easy

Kogane Fern, which turns red in the fall, adds a nice touch to this moss ball.

Aitade

Persicaria tinctoria

▶ Polygonaceae, Persicaria (Annual plant)

Also called Japanese Indigo. Native to China and South East Asia. It was traditionally used for making indigo dye. During fall, the upright stems sprout deep pink flowers.

SOIL Soil with good drainage **LIGHTING** Plenty of light and air circulation. Keep in partial shade during summer. **BLOOMING** September to November **WATERING** When the moss ball becomes light, add water. **DIFFICULTY** Average

Common Japanese Moss Balls

The plant at the Katsura base is a type of small clover.

The small plant at the base is called Tatsunamisou. It has little white flowers that bloom in spring to early summer.

Katsura

Cercidiphyllum japonicum

Cercidiphyllaceae, Cercidiphylum
(Deciduous plant)

Common all over Japan. It has rounded heart-shaped leaves and is especially beautiful when new green leaves sprout. The leaves turn yellow in the fall. While not a particularly large plant, it can still get fairly big, so prune as needed.

SOIL Soil with good drainage **LIGHTING** Plenty of light and air circulation. Keep in partial shade during summer. **BLOOMING** A red-threadlike flower blooms around May **WATERING** Once per day **DIFFICULTY** Average

Hozakinanakamado

Sorbaria sorbifolia

Rosaceae, Sorbaria (Deciduous shrub)

Also called False Spirea, this species is common all over Japan. The narrow leaves forming fronds on the branches is one of its unique traits. During early summer, panicles of tiny white flowers will blossom. During fall the leaves turn red.

SOIL Soil with good drainage **LIGHTING** Plenty of light and air circulation. Keep in partial shade during summer. **BLOOMING** September to October **WATERING** Once per day **DIFFICULTY** Easy

Four Seasons Yunnan Hagi

◀ Fabaceae, Lespedeza (Deciduous shrub)

This China native is from the *Lespedeza* genus. During spring to fall little pink beads of flowers bloom. It's a sturdy plant and easy to handle.

SOIL Soil with good drainage **LIGHTING** Sunny to half-shaded. Keep in partial shade during summer. **BLOOMING** March to April **WATERING** When the moss ball becomes light, add water. **DIFFICULTY** Easy

Left Combined with the yellow-flowered Himetsuwabuki. Adding some driftwood like so, gives it some more life.

Aburachan

Lindera praecox

▶ Lauraceae, Lindera (Decidous shrub)

Common in mountainous areas all over Japan. The flower is yellow, and the leaves turn red. You can try combining it with a plant that complements the shape of the branches.

SOIL Soil with good drainage **LIGHTING** Keep in partial shade **BLOOMING** March to April **WATERING** Water generously once daily. **DIFFICULTY** Easy

Right The Nobudou is often used as a bottom combination plant. During early Fall, the leaves are purple.

Sanchou

Zanthoxylum piperitum

◀ Rutaceae, Zanthoxylum (Decidous shrub)

Also called Japanese Pepper. Native to Japan and the Korean Peninsula. It was traditionally used to add fragrance to foods. Avoid extreme dryness.

SOIL Soil with good drainage **LIGHTING** Plenty of light and air circulation. Keep in partial shade during summer. **BLOOMING** March to April **WATERING** Once per day **DIFFICULTY** Easy

Left The variation in the image has yellow spotted leaves.

Ezomatsu

Karamatsu

Enoki

Karamatsu

Larix kaempferi

Pinaceae, Larix (Decidous Tree)

Also called the Japanese Larch. Because the roots grow quickly, it is often planted in the cold highlands of Japan. It is a rare pine that sheds leaves. It should be kept slightly dry.

SOIL Soil with good drainage **LIGHTING** Plenty of light and air circulation. Keep in partial shade during summer. **BLOOMING** May **WATERING** When the moss ball becomes light, add water. When the moss becomes too dry, spray to give moisture. **DIFFICULTY** Average

Ezomatsu

Picea jezoensis

Pinaceae, Picea (Evergreen plant)

Also called the Ezo Spruce. Bonsai gardeners will be familiar with this plant, which is often found in cold regions in the Northern Hemisphere. Its bark is dark brown. It is possible to grow it in warm areas, but be careful of dry conditions, as this plant prefers dampness. To maintain the shape, pick sprouts annually.

SOIL Soil with good drainage **LIGHTING** Plenty of light and air circulation. Keep in partial shade during summer. **WATERING** Water generously once daily. **DIFFICULTY** Average

Enoki

Chamaecyparis obtusa

Cupressaceae, Chamaecyparis (Evergreen plant)

Also called Hinoki Cypress, this tree is common in all regions in Japan, where its wood is a very popular high-end building material. It is often used in bonsai, and works equally well for moss balls.

SOIL Soil with good drainage **LIGHTING** Plenty of light and air circulation. Keep in partial shade during summer. **WATERING** When the moss ball becomes light, add plenty of water. **DIFFICULTY** Easy

The variation in the image is a Renzan Enoki, which has very dense leaves and branches, requiring a lot of good light and ventilation

Inubiwa

Ficus erecta
▶ Ficeae, Ficus (deciduous plant)

Also called Japanese Fig. This plant produces elongated green leaves and edible little figs.

SOIL Soil with good drainage **LIGHTING** Sunny to half-shaded, and air circulation. Keep in partial shade during summer. **BLOOMING** April to May **WATERING** When the moss ball becomes light, add plenty of water. **DIFFICULTY** Easy

Kuromatsu

Pinus thunbergii
◀ Pinaceae, Pinus (Evergreen plant)

Also called Japanese Pine or Japanese Black Pine. Another traditional bonsai plant, this is often seen all over Japan's seasides. The trunks are black and its needles can be copious.

SOIL Soil with good drainage **LIGHTING** Sunny to half-shaded, and air circulation. Keep in partial shade during summer. **WATERING** When the moss ball becomes light, add plenty of water. **DIFFICULTY** Easy

Cranberry

◀ Ericaceae, Vaccinium (Evergreen shrub)

Native to the cold regions in the Northern Hemisphere, the fruits are familiar to most. The berries are yellow in the growing stages, and by fall, the color deepens and eventually turns red (see p. 23). Favors moist conditions.

SOIL Soil with good drainage **LIGHTING** Plenty of light and air circulation. Keep in partial shade during summer. **BLOOMING** May to June **WATERING** Water generously once daily. You can keep wet mizugoke at the bottom of the plate for plenty of moisture. **DIFFICULTY** Average

Yanbaruganpi

Wikstroemia indica

▸ Thymelaeaceae, Wikstroemia (Evergreen shrub)

Also called Indian Stringbush. Naturally grows in Okinawa and South East Asia. At one time, this plant was used for making paper. The color changes from green to orange to red. Prefers a warm climate.

SOIL Soil with good drainage **LIGHTING** Plenty of light and air circulation. Keep in partial shade during summer. **BLOOMING** May to October **WATERING** When the moss ball becomes light, add plenty of water. **DIFFICULTY** Average

Hazelnut

◂ Anacardiaceae, Toxicodendron (Deciduous plant)

Native to East and South East Asia. New leaves grow during spring and the leaves turn red in the fall (see p. 23). People with sensitive skin should be careful when handling this plant.

SOIL Soil with good drainage **LIGHTING** Plenty of light and air circulation. Keep in partial shade during summer. **WATERING** When the moss ball becomes light, add water. **DIFFICULTY** Easy

Keyaki

Zelkova serrata

▸ Ulmaceae, Zelkova (Deciduous plant)

Also called Japanese Zelkova. This is another bonsai favorite that is common in all regions of Japan. When it grows larger, the leaves fan out. In the forest, this tree serves as a buffer against wind. It is vulnerable to exhaust fumes, so it may not be suited to urban envroinments.

SOIL Soil with good drainage **LIGHTING** Plenty of light and air circulation. Keep in partial shade during summer. **BLOOMING** April to May **WATERING** When the moss ball becomes light, add plenty of water. **DIFFICULTY** Easy

The leaves in fall.

Mayumi
Euonymus hamiltonianus
◀ Calastraceae, Euonymus (Deciduous plant)

Also called the Himalayan Spindle, it's common in all regions in Japan and the Korean Peninsula. It has a unique characteristic of sqaurish fruit hanging from the branches. The fruit ranges from whitish to vermillion to deep red during the fall.

SOIL Soil with good drainage **LIGHTING** Sunny to half-shaded, and air circulation. Keep in partial shade during summer. **BLOOMING** May to June **WATERING** When the moss ball becomes light, add plenty of water. **DIFFICULTY** Easy

Pink flowers with red seeds.

Hatsuyukikazura
Trachelospermum asiaticum 'Hatsuyukikazura'
▶ Apocynaceae, Trachelospermum (Evergreen shrub)

Common in the main and Kyushu islands of Japan. This is a vine type of plant. The new stems are light pink. When it grows out signficantly, trim as needed.

SOIL Soil with good drainage **LIGHTING** Sunny to half-shaded, and air circulation. Keep in partial shade during summer. **BLOOMING** May to June **WATERING** When the moss ball becomes light, add plenty of water. **DIFFICULTY** Average

Japanese Maple
◀ Sapindaceae, Acer (Deciduous plant)

This is another bonsai favorite. You can enjoy this plant all year round, from the changing fall leaves to the fresh new leaves.

SOIL Soil with good drainage **LIGHTING** Plenty of light and air circulation. Keep in partial shade during summer. **BLOOMING** Approximately in April **WATERING** Water generously once daily. **DIFFICULTY** Easy

Kamatsuka
Photinia villosa
◀ Rasaceae, Pourthiaea (Deciduous shrub)

Native to Japan, Korea, and China. The white flowers are followed by fall berries that last into early winter, earning this shrub the nickname Christmas Berry. You'll also see beautiful fall foliage from October to November.

SOIL Soil with good drainage **LIGHTING** Plenty of light and air circulation. Keep in partial shade during summer. **BLOOMING** April to May **WATERING** Water generously once daily. **DIFFICULTY** Easy

Left This is a combination of a one-year old, early-blooming Kamatsuka, and a white flower Hakone Chrysanthemum.

Chinese Tallow
Triadica sebifera
▶ Euphorbiaceae, Triadica (Deciduous plant)

Native to China, this plant grows well in warmer North American climates. It has a rounded water-drop-shaped leaf. It comes into its own during the fall.

SOIL Soil with good drainage **LIGHTING** Plenty of light and air circulation. Keep in partial shade during summer. **BLOOMING** May to June **WATERING** When the moss ball becomes light, add plenty of water. **DIFFICULTY** Easy

Right Paired up with Asamarindo, whose flower blooms in the fall.

Shiroshikibu
Callicarpa f. alibibacca Beautyberry
◀ Lamiaceae, Callicarpa (Deciduous shrub)

Common around East Asia. This is a short plant with a purple fruit. During the first weeks of summer, you'll see white flowers blooming, then around October to November little fruits appear. When the plant becomes large, the branches usually bend.

SOIL Soil with good drainage **LIGHTING** Plenty of light and air circulation. Keep in partial shade during summer. **BLOOMING** June to July **WATERING** Water generously once daily **DIFFICULTY** Easy

Left Paired with Checkerberry, which adds red color to your moss ball in fall to winter

Grass and Herb Moss Balls

Fuuchisou

Hakonechloa macra

Poaceae, Hakonechloa (Perennial plant)

A Japanese grass plant in the Poaceae family, this is a bonsai classic. Its leaves are narrow and long, and very relaxing to watch as the breeze catches them. It wilts in winter but revives in spring.

SOIL Soil with good drainage **LIGHTING** Keep in a partial shade **BLOOMING** August to October **WATERING** Water generously once daily. You can keep wet mizugoke at the bottom of the plate for plenty of moisture **DIFFICULTY** Easy

Right There are a number different types to work with.

Giboushi

Hosta

Asparagaceae, Hosta (Perennial plant)

Native to East Asia and grows well in temperate climates. There are many types, showing variations in leaf color and leaf pattern. This is one plant that loves staying in the shade. In the mountain forests, it usually grows in the wetlands. The flower stem grows out straight. It wilts during winter, but grows back out in spring.

SOIL Soil with good drainage **LIGHTING** Keep in a partial shade and air circulation **BLOOMING** June to August **WATERING** Water generously once daily. **DIFFICULTY** Easy

★ The plant in this image is the Moonlight variation.

Chinese Virginia Creeper

Vitaceae, Parthenocissus (Deciduous creeper)

Native to China. It's very tolerant and easy to raise. It is also often used to cover up walls and grounds. Usually the leaves turn red in the fall. When the vine grows long, trim at the tips. You can use a pin to attach the vines to the moss ball—it will grow roots.

SOIL Soil with good drainage **LIGHTING** Plenty of light and air circulation. Keep in partial shade during summer. **BLOOMING** April to May **WATERING** When the moss ball becomes light, add water. **DIFFICULTY** Easy

Right Combined with Violet at the main stem.

Amadokoro

Polygonatum odoratum

▶ Asparagaceae, Polygonatum (Perennial plant)

Also called Solomon's Seal. The stem arches as it grows. When spring comes along, white flowers bloom from the base of the leaves. It can be healthily raised in the shade. The top portion wilts during winter.

SOIL Soil with good drainage **LIGHTING** Keep a in partial shade with air circulation **BLOOMING** April to June **WATERING** When the moss ball becomes light, add plenty of water. **DIFFICULTY** Easy

★ **Here is a variation with yellow streaks.**

Creeping Raspberry

◀ Rosaceae, Rubus (Evergreen shrub)

Native to the temperate zones of the Northern Hemisphere. An attractive plant that's relative to raspberries. The plant will fruit during summer. A very resilient plant, it's also used as ground cover.

SOIL Soil with good drainage **LIGHTING** Sunny to half-shaded and air circulation. Keep in partial shade during summer. **BLOOMING** May to June **WATERING** When the moss ball becomes light, add water. **DIFFICULTY** Easy

Himewatasuge

Trichophorum alpinum (L.) Persoon

▶ Cyperaceae, Scirpus (Perennial plant)

Also called Alpine Bullrush. Distributed in Hokkaido wetlands, and parts of the Northern Hemisphere. After flowering, you can see cottony tips at the ends. Imagine it swaying in the summer breeze!

SOIL Soil with good drainage **LIGHTING** Plenty of light and air circulation. Keep in partial shade during summer. **BLOOMING** June to August **WATERING** Water generously once daily. You can keep wet mizugoke at the bottom of the plate for plenty of moisture. **DIFFICULTY** Average

Nioihange

Yashazenmai

Jasmine

Yashazenmai

Osmunda lancea
Osmundaceae, Osmunda

Can be seen in rocky mountain streams. It prefers moist conditions. When the leaves open up, you can see a nice green color. The moss used in this image is Thuidium (see p. 29, 49). The top portion withers away in winter, so it is nice to pair it up with an evergreen.

SOIL Soil with good drainage **LIGHTING** Keep in a half-shaded to shaded and warm place **WATERING** Water generously once daily. You can keep wet mizugoke at the bottom of the plate for plenty of moisture. **DIFFICULTY** Average

Nioihange

Pinellia cordata
Araceae, Pinellia (Perennial plant)

Native to China. The leaves have a distinguished shape and a faint fragrance.

SOIL Soil with good drainage **LIGHTING** Keep in a half-shaded place **BLOOMING** May to August **WATERING** Water generously once daily. **DIFFICULTY** Average

Jasmine

Oleaceae, Jasminum (Evergreen shrub)

Known to have hundreds of varieties. The flower can be white or yellow, with a lilting floral scent. After flowering, some pruning will be needed. It can be divided and cloned for a new plant.

SOIL Soil with good drainage **LIGHTING** Plenty of light and air circulation. Keep in partial shade during summer. **BLOOMING** April to October (depending on the type) **WATERING** When the moss becomes light, add plenty of water. **DIFFICULTY** Easy

★ **This is the Fiona Sunrise Jasmine (Gold-leaved Jasmine).**

Aztec Sweet Herb
▶ Verbanaceae, Phyla (Perennial plant)

Native to Central America. Its charm increases as the branches and leaves grow out. If you make this into an herb tea, you wouldn't need to add any sugar. It is a resilient plant, easy to raise.

SOIL Soil with good drainage **LIGHTING** Plenty of light and air circulation. Keep in partial shade during summer. **BLOOMING** June to August **WATERING** When the moss becomes light, add plenty of water. **DIFFICULTY** Easy

Swiss Chard
▶ Chenopodiaceae, Beta (Perennial plant)

Swiss chard can be distinguished by its colorful stem. There are red, gold, and white-stem varieties. It is a visually admirable vegetable! Often used in salads, it's also nice in a moss ball.

SOIL Soil with good drainage **LIGHTING** Plenty of light and air circulation. Keep in partial shade during summer. **WATERING** When the moss becomes light, add plenty of water. **DIFFICULTY** Easy

Rosemary
◀ Lamiaceae, Rosmarinus (Evergreen shrub)

Can be found along the seaside. This grassy herb scents the air with a wonderful, clean fragrance. There are upright types as well as creeping types. It can grow quite strong, but be careful of excess moisture.

SOIL Soil with good drainage **LIGHTING** Plenty of light and air circulation. Keep in partial shade during summer. **BLOOMING** April to November **WATERING** When the moss becomes light, add plenty of water. **DIFFICULTY** Easy

Water Pennyworts

Himetokusa

Kuwai

Above Kuwai is placed on the left. It is combined with another swamp plant, Akebonoashi. Two moss balls combined together, resembling camel humps.

Water Pennyworts

Araliaceae, Hydrocotyle
(Perennial plant)

Native to North America. It prefers full sun and a wet growing environment. Its round shaped leaves is unique and easy to spot. It can grow quite sturdily, but be sure to give it adequate moisture.

SOIL Soil with good drainage **LIGHTING** Plenty of light and air circulation. Keep in partial shade during summer. **BLOOMING** June to September **WATERING** Water generously once daily. You can keep wet mizugoke at the bottom of the plate for plenty of moisture. **DIFFICULTY** Average

Himetokusa

Equisetum variegatum

Equisetaceae, Equisetum
(Perennial plant)

Also called Variegated Horsetail. Native to the northern part of the Northern Hemisphere. Compared to horsetail grass, it has finer leaves. Give plenty of moisture.

SOIL Soil with good drainage **LIGHTING** Keep in a half-shaded to shaded place. **WATERING** Water generously once daily. You can keep wet mizugoke at the bottom of the plate for plenty of moisture. **DIFFICULTY** Easy

Kuwai

Sagittaria trifolia L. 'Caerulea'

Alismataceae, Sagittaria
(Perennial plant)

Also called Threeleaf Arrowhead. This plant pretty much lives in the water. This plant produces an edible tuber, and the leaf has been used for medicinal purposes.

SOIL Soil with good drainage **LIGHTING** Plenty of light and air circulation. Keep in partial shade during summer. **WATERING** Water generously once daily. You can keep wet mizugoke at the bottom of the plate for plenty of moisture. **DIFFICULTY** Difficult

Foliage, Succulents and Other Moss Balls

Asparagus
Asparagaceae, Asparagus (Perennial plant)

There are many types of Asparagus in the tropical and sub-tropical climates. It's the same species as the one we eat, but it's also used as a decorative plant. It's relatively resistant to dryness. Be aware of excess moisture.

SOIL Soil with good drainage **LIGHTING** Plenty of light and air circulation. Keep in partial shade during summer. **BLOOMING** June to July **WATERING** When the moss becomes light, add plenty of water. **DIFFICULTY** Easy

★ The variation in the image is a popular variation, the Lace Fern.

Pachira
Bombacoideae, Pachira (Evergreen plant)

Native to tropical Asia. This is a popular house plant, known for its five-leaf arrangement. It's resistant to cold weather. A very sturdy, healthy plant, perfect for beginners.

SOIL Soil with good drainage **LIGHTING** Plenty of light and air circulation. Keep in partial shade during summer. **WATERING** When the moss becomes light, add plenty of water. **DIFFICULTY** Easy

Dwarf Schefflera Umbrella Tree
▶ Araliaceae, Schefflera (Evergreen plant)

Many types can be found in the tropical zones. This is a very popular house plant. It has deep green leaves, and a beautiful arrangement. It's a sturdy plant, easy to grow.

SOIL Soil with good drainage **LIGHTING** Plenty of light and air circulation. Keep in partial shade during summer. **WATERING** When the moss becomes light, add plenty of water. **DIFFICULTY** Easy

★ The type in the image has a shallow cut in the leaves, *Schefflera arboricola* 'Renate.'

Begonia

Begoniaceae, Begonia
(Perennial plant)

There are many types found in the tropical climates around the world. They are popular as potted plants both indoors and outdoors. Some varieties are ever-blooming.

SOIL Soil with good drainage **LIGHTING** Keep in a half-shaded place **BLOOMING** April to November **WATERING** When the moss becomes light, add plenty of water. **DIFFICULTY** Average

★ Even though this is a grove plant type, it is often considered a succulent.

Fern

Adiantaceae, Adiantum
(Perennial plant)

You can see this growing everywhere in the wild. The stems are nearly black, giving it a nice contrast. Another popular houseplant.

SOIL Soil with good drainage **LIGHTING** Plenty of light and air circulation. Keep in partial shade during summer. **WATERING** When the moss becomes light, add plenty of water. When the moss dries up too quickly, spray to moisturize. **DIFFICULTY** Average

Weeping Fig

Moraceae, Ficus
(Evergreen plant)

Popular as a house plant. When its environment changes, the leaves may fall. However, they will grow back when the tree adjusts to its new environment.

SOIL Soil with good drainage **LIGHTING** Plenty of light and air circulation. Keep in partial shade during summer. **WATER-ING** When the moss becomes light, add plenty of water. **DIFFICULTY** Average

★ In the image is a spotted type of weeping fig.

Maidenhair Fern

◀ Adiantaceae, Adiantum (Perennial plant)

Well-known plant in the tropical and sub-tropical zones. It dislikes dryness, and will wilt, so make sure to keep it moist at all times.

SOIL Soil with good drainage **LIGHTING** Keep in a half-shaded place **WATERING** Water generously once daily. Giving moisture to the leaves by spraying is also recommended. You can keep wet mizugoke at the bottom of the plate for plenty of moisture. **DIFFICULTY** Average

Here, it is paired with a larger type of the same species, for contrast.

Shinobu

Davallia mariesii

▶ Davalliaceae, Davallia (Perennial plant)

Distributed throughout Japan, China, and Korea. This is a plant that grows on other plants. Enhance its charm by hanging it from the ceiling. It dries out faster when suspended, so make sure to monitor closely.

SOIL Soil with good drainage or using mizugoke is already recommended **LIGHTING** Keep in a half-shaded to shaded place **WATERING** Once or twice per day, spray the leaves to keep them moist **DIFFICULTY** Average

Right Davallia (Western Shinobu) moss ball and a Bat Orchid moss ball hanging from each other.

Hidakamisebaya

Sedum cauticola

◀ Crassulaceae, Hylotelephium (Perennial plant)

A succulent native to Japan. It's a small plant, good for small spaces. The round leaves face each other as they grow. The leaves become red during the fall, when tiny raspberry red flowers bloom.

SOIL Soil with good drainage **LIGHTING** Plenty of light and air circulation. Keep in partial shade during summer. **BLOOMING** October to November **WATERING** When the moss becomes light, add plenty of water. **DIFFICULTY** Easy

Left Combination with tall and short Shiran (*Bletilla striata*).

Aloe

▶ Asphodelaceae, Aloe (Perennial plant)

A well-known succulent native to Africa and Madagascar. There are many variations. This plant is often used for medicinal purposes. When picking up at the store, make sure to choose one with sturdy leaves and a firm stem.

SOIL Soil with good drainage **LIGHTING** Plenty of light and air circulation. Keep in partial shade during summer. **BLOOMING** December to March **WATERING** When the moss becomes light, add water. If the moss dries up quick, spray to give moisture to the moss. **DIFFICULTY** Easy

Right To the right is a combination with other succulent plants. At the bottom is a *Haworthia cooperi* moss ball. Combining in this way makes it easy to maintain the amount of moisture given since these plants are compatible.

Kangaroo Pocket

Kusahanabi

Dashiakansa

Kusahanabi

Talinum calycinum
Talinaceae, Talinum

Commonly called Fame Flower, this succulent is native to North America. It has a long slender stem with flowers at the tips. The flower opens during the afternoon from mid-spring until the first frost. Be careful of excess moisture.

SOIL Soil with good drainage **LIGHTING** Plenty of light and air circulation. Keep in partial shade during summer. **BLOOMING** July to September **WATERING** When the moss becomes light, add water. **DIFFICULTY** Average

Kangaroo Pocket

Asclepiadaceae, Dischidia
(Perennial plant)

Common in Southeast Asia and the Pacific islands. Some of the leaves will swell up and become water reservoirs, giving this plant a unique look. It has small red flowers. The root is vulnerable to too much moisture, so keep that in mind when watering.

SOIL Soil with good drainage **LIGHTING** Plenty of light and air circulation. Keep in partial shade during summer. **BLOOMING** June to August **WATERING** When the moss becomes light, add water. If the moss dries up quick, spray to give moisture to the moss. **DIFFICULTY** Difficult

Dashiakansa

Mammillaria laui ssp. *dasyacantha*
Cactaceae, Mammillaria

Native in Central America. It is tiny, and the flowers keep blooming. You can often see this cactus at the store.

SOIL Soil with good drainage **LIGHTING** Sunny to half-shaded place. Keep in half-shaded place during summer **BLOOMING** March to May **WATERING** Soak in water once every 5 days. Spray to give moisture to the moss. **DIFFICULTY** Average

Mimikakigusa

Utricularia bifida

▶ Lentibulariaceae, Utricularia (Perennial/Annual plant)

Found in the world's wetlands. *Utricularia*, commony called Bladderwort, is a caniverous genus with over 200 species. It loves moisture, so make sure to keep this moss ball constantly moist.

SOIL Soil mixed with mizugoke, or just mizugoke is recommended **LIGHTING** Plenty of light and air circulation. Keep in partial shade during summer. **BLOOMING** May to July **WATERING** Water generously once daily. Giving moisture to the leaves by spraying is also recommended. You can keep wet mizugoke at the bottom of the plate for plenty of moisture. **DIFFICULTY** Average

The variation in the image is called 'Clione' from Clionidae. It is also sometimes called Bunny Moss.

Haetorigusa Venus Flytrap

◀ Droseraceae, Dionaea (Perennial plant)

A carnivorous plant from North America. The leaves are hairy inside. When touched, they shut tight. Make sure not to handle or play around with the leaves too much, because it will drain the plant's energy, which can cause the leaves to wilt. It can live without eating insects.

SOIL Soil with good drainage **LIGHTING** Plenty of light and air circulation. Keep in partial shade during summer. **BLOOMING** May to July **WATERING** Water generously once daily. Giving moisture to the leaves by spraying is also recommended. You can keep wet mizugoke at the bottom of the plate for plenty of moisture. **DIFFICULTY** Average

Climacium Japonicum

▶ Climaciaceae, Climacium (Perennial plant)

Larger types of moss can be used as the plant in moss balls. This is a Japanese moss that grows on wet grounds (see p. 51). Here, we combined with Thuidium. You can also raise this moss ball in a glass container.

SOIL Soil with good drainage **LIGHTING** Keep in a half-shaded place **WATERING** Water generously once daily. Giving moisture to the leaves by spraying is also recommended. You can keep wet mizugoke at the bottom of the plate for plenty of moisture. **DIFFICULTY** Average

Index to the Mosses and Plants

Published by Tuttle Publishing, an imprint of Periplus Editions (HK) Ltd.

www.tuttlepublishing.com

ISBN 978-4-8053-1529-3

Kokedama to Koke Sodatekata Note
Copyright © Satoshi Sunamori 2014
English translation rights arranged with IE-NO-HIKARI ASSOCIATION through Japan UNI Agency, Inc., Tokyo

English Translation ©2020 Periplus Editions (HK) Ltd.
Translated from Japanese by HL Language Services

Original Japanese edition
Design Yo Yamamoto, Kana Sugai (yohdel)
Photography Akiyoshi Yamamoto, Mizuki Karube
Illustrations Yo Yamamoto
Proofreader Hiroko Sato
Images courtesy of Studio Te, Nishiogi Department Store

Distributed by
North America, Latin America & Europe
Tuttle Publishing
364 Innovation Drive
North Clarendon, VT 05759-9436 U.S.A.
Tel: (802) 773-8930; Fax: (802) 773-6993
info@tuttlepublishing.com; www.tuttlepublishing.com

Japan
Tuttle Publishing
Yaekari Building 3rd Floor
5-4-12 Osaki
Shinagawa-ku, Tokyo 141-0032
Tel: (81) 3 5437-0171; Fax: (81) 3 5437-0755
sales@tuttle.co.jp; www.tuttle.co.jp

Asia Pacific
Berkeley Books Pte. Ltd.
3 Kallang Sector #04-01, Singapore 349278
Tel: (65) 6741-2178; Fax: (65) 6741-2179
inquiries@periplus.com.sg; www.tuttlepublishing.com

Printed in Hong Kong   2001EP
24 23 22 21 20   10 9 8 7 6 5 4 3 2 1

TUTTLE PUBLISHING® is a registered trademark of Tuttle Publishing, a division of Periplus Editions (HK) Ltd.

The Tuttle Story
"Books to Span the East and West"

Our core mission at Tuttle Publishing is to create books which bring people together one page at a time. Tuttle was founded in 1832 in the small New England town of Rutland, Vermont (USA). Our fundamental values remain as strong today as they were then—to publish best-in-class books informing the English-speaking world about the countries and peoples of Asia. The world has become a smaller place today and Asia's economic, cultural and political influence has expanded, yet the need for meaningful dialogue and information about this diverse region has never been greater. Since 1948, Tuttle has been a leader in publishing books on the cultures, arts, cuisines, languages and literatures of Asia. Our authors and photographers have won numerous awards and Tuttle has published thousands of books on subjects ranging from martial arts to paper crafts. We welcome you to explore the wealth of information available on Asia at **www.tuttlepublishing.com.**